MY PONY SCRAPBOOK

Rebekah Taylor Pascoe

HI!

My name is Rebekah Taylor Pascoe, but everyone calls me Becky. This is me with my pony Chance. I'm in my pony club uniform.

Horse
galloping

This pony scrapbook is all about horses and ponies, and how to take care of them. It's got pictures of Chance and me, and pictures of other horses as well.

Chance and me at home

A mare with her foal

CONTENTS

About Ponies and Horses

DID YOU KNOW?

Horses are herbivores, which means they spend their day looking for and eating grass.

The saddle sits on a horse's back. Horses and ponies need their saddles fitted by a special person to make sure they fit comfortably on their back.

Never let your pony get too fat on spring grass or they will get laminitis (that means they become too fat and can't walk properly).

Horses are measured in 'hands'. One hand is equal to 10 centimetres (4 inches) and horses are measured from their wither to the ground. Any horse under 14.2 hands is called a pony. Horses that are 14.2 hands or higher are called horses. Chance is 12.2 hands high, which means she is a pony.

I love Chance!

Neigh! Neigh!

Forelock
Poll
Ear
Crest
Neck
Shoulder
Mane
Back
Flank
Rump
Forehead
Wither
Loins
Dock
Eye
Nose
Cheek
Cheekbone
Nostril
Muzzle
Tail
Mouth
Chest
Thigh
Hock
Elbow
Belly
Gaskin
Knee
Pastern
Fetlock
Cannon bone
Coronet
Heel
Wall of hoof

HERE ARE ALL THE
PARTS OF A HORSE.

Horny
wall of
hoof
Coronary
band
Toe
Heel
Frog
Wall
Sole
White line

PARTS OF A HOOF

2

WHAT YOU NEED FOR RIDING

HERE IS A LIST OF THINGS YOU WILL NEED FOR RIDING:

A helmet that fits really well.

♥

Jodhpurs (riding trousers).

♥

Special riding boots (they can be long or short).

This is me holding my bridle and saddle. I got my saddle for Christmas last year.

HERE IS A LIST OF THINGS YOUR PONY WILL NEED:

A saddle (with a girth, stirrups and stirrup leathers).

♥

A saddle cloth.

♥

A bridle (with a bit and reins).

bridle

saddle

saddle cloth

reins

bit

stirrup leather

stirrup

girth

GETTING A PONY

IF YOU ARE LUCKY LIKE ME, YOU MIGHT LIVE ON A SMALL FARM. BUT IF YOU DON'T, YOU WILL HAVE TO RENT A PADDOCK FOR YOUR PONY.

WHAT KIND OF PADDOCK YOU WILL NEED:

It should be at least the size of two Olympic swimming pools.

It should have plenty of shade (maybe even a shelter).

It should have grass (but you will need to feed your pony hay in winter).

It should have fresh water.

It should be safe (no holes, or old wire and tin, good fences).

IF YOU WANT TO BUY A PONY, YOU CAN:

* Ask some people from the local pony club if they know of any good ponies that are safe to ride.
* Look for a pony in the paper or in a horse magazine.

REMEMBER!

* When you go to look at the pony, make sure you take someone with you who knows all about horses.
*If you like the pony, you should ask the owners if you can take it home for a trial (that means you can try the pony for a while without buying it).
*And before you buy the pony, have a vet check it to see that it is 'sound' (that means there is nothing wrong with it).

HOW TO RIDE

You should never hold your reins too tight and too short because that will hurt your pony's mouth. If you have your reins too loose, you won't be able to steer your pony.

You need to remember to:
* sit up straight
* look between your pony's ears
* keep your heels down
* keep the balls of your feet on the stirrups
* keep your legs nice and firm on your pony's sides

This is a picture of me when I first started to ride. I was 4 years old. I am riding a very old pony called Tiffy. Sometimes Mum had to lead me! How embarrassing!

You have to TRY to remember to hold your reins correctly. This means you have to keep your thumbs up and on top of the reins with your fingers gripping them and your little fingers below the reins. Here is a drawing of how it looks when you get it right.

This is a picture of a really good rider. She is sitting in the correct position for riding. She makes it look easy but when your pony is going really fast, it isn't always easy to remember everything you've learnt!!!

Horses
have four paces:
* walk
* trot
* canter
* gallop (that's really,
really fast).

Learning to trot on a pony is pretty tricky and takes time to learn. You have to go up and down in the saddle as the pony trots. But you have to keep your hands and legs still. They don't go up and down — only your bottom does!

You should only canter when you are sure you are balanced (that means you don't slip from side to side in the saddle).

RIDING

Learning to ride is not easy. It takes lots of practice. But when you can walk, trot and canter by yourself, and you don't fall off, it is an awesome feeling!!!

Taking care of your pony

FOOD

♥ Most ponies live in a paddock. They need:
* grass
* water
* shade
* hay in winter

♥ If you are riding your pony lots and lots, you might need to give them some special pony mix. It is usually made up of chaff, oats and vitamins. It gives your pony much more energy.

Delicious!

Yum! Yum!

Because there isn't a lot of grass around in winter you will need to feed your pony some hay.

WORMING YOUR PONY

You should always worm your pony every 6 to 8 weeks with worming paste or a worming powder (you can get this from your local vet or produce store).

This horse needs to be wormed and put in a fresh paddock with lots of good grass.

IMPORTANT!!!

It is really important to worm your pony. Horses can get all kinds of worms and they can make your pony feel really sick. A pony with worms will have a dull coat and will often look thin and unhappy.

RUGS

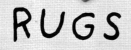

Because Chance is white, she wears a light cotton rug in summer to keep her coat clean.

In winter she has a nice warm waterproof rug.

If it is cold where you live, you will probably have to rug your pony in winter.

Make sure the rug is waterproof and comfortable and it doesn't rub your pony anywhere.

Chance in her winter rug

Here is a picture of me
brushing Chance

GROOMING

Ponies need to be brushed
often. It keeps their skin
and coat clean and healthy.

You should always brush
your pony before you
ride and after you have
finished riding.

You need to brush
your pony all over but
especially where the
bridle and saddle go.
It's really uncomfortable
for your pony if there
is some mud or dirt
under the girth or the
saddle cloth.

Hooves

Ponies' hooves are very important. If you are riding on stones or dirt roads, you will probably need to get shoes put on your pony.

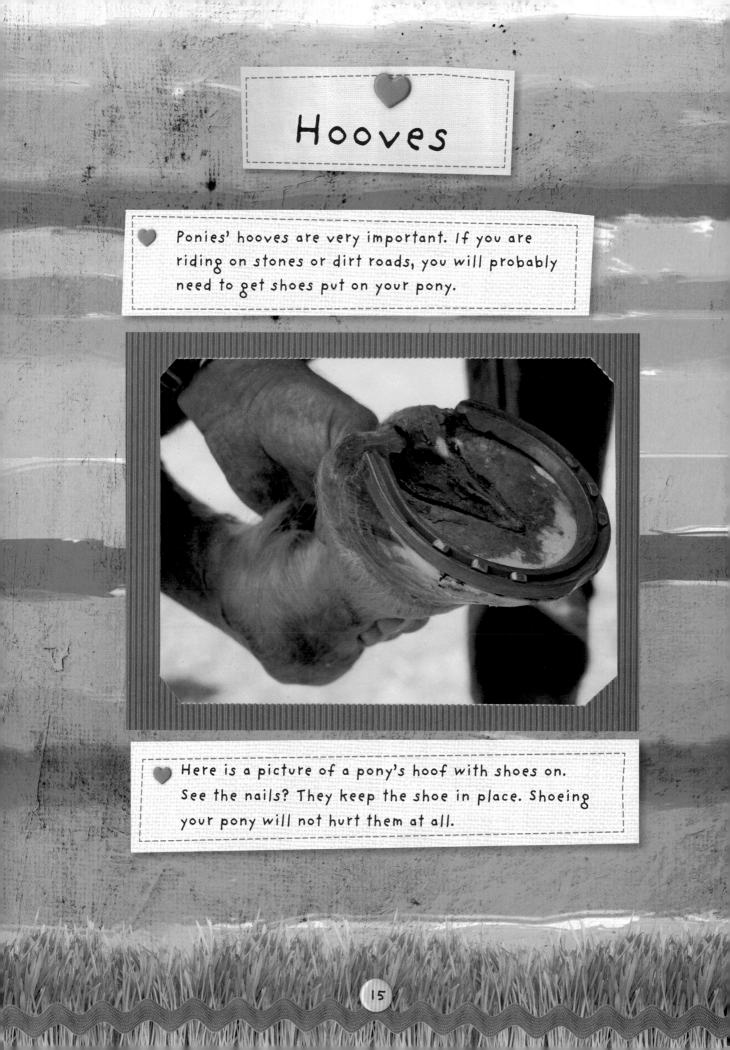

Here is a picture of a pony's hoof with shoes on. See the nails? They keep the shoe in place. Shoeing your pony will not hurt them at all.

Horse shoes are made of iron and are shaped to fit your pony's hoof. Every 6 to 8 weeks the shoes have to come off and your pony's hooves need to be trimmed (just like you need to cut your toenails). Then the shoes are put back on again.

A person who shoes horses is called a farrier. Some horses don't wear shoes but they still need to have their hooves trimmed every 6 to 8 weeks.

This is a picture of Don. He is a farrier. He is trimming Chance's hooves. Chance does not need shoes because she has really tough hooves.

REMEMBER!!!

Before and after you go for a ride, make sure you use a hoof pick to clean out any stones and dirt in your pony's hooves.

GOING TO PONY CLUB

white shirt

green tie and pony club badge

pony club jumper

medical armband

beige jodhpurs

brown elastic-sided riding boots

I started pony club when I was eight years old. Pony club is held once a month and is heaps of fun! We are all put into groups. There are six groups at my pony club. The beginners are in Group 6, but I am in Group 5.

This is me in full pony club uniform.

17

GROUP 5

OUR INSTRUCTOR, APRIL, AND ME

ASHLEIGH ON SPRITE

SAMANTHA ON DUNDEE

JESSE ON CASPER

AIDAN ON SAMMY

A DAY AT PONY CLUB

This is Brooke. She is an instructor at my pony club.

9.30am
Gear Check

This is where my instructor for the day checks that Chance's saddle and bridle are fitting properly and nothing is broken.

The instructor also checks that I have on the correct helmet and boots, that I am wearing my medical armband, and that I am in full pony club uniform.

10.00am to 11.00am
Flat Riding

Our instructor makes us ride round and round a flat area called a dressage arena. As we ride around she tells us how we should be sitting or holding our hands, or where our legs should be.

Sometimes we do a dressage test, where we might walk, trot or canter between letters on signs in the arena.

11.00am to 12.00pm
Show Jumping

Show jumping is my favourite thing to do. The instructor puts up about seven jumps and we have to go over them one after the other. You have to be careful to remember where to go, and that your pony doesn't knock down any jumps.

The jumping position is different to normal riding. You have to lean forward and shorten your reins as you push your pony over the jump. Jumping is an amazing feeling! Just like flying!

This is a picture of me with a trophy and Chance with a red ribbon.
We won them at the Pony Club Challenge. It is a competition that is held in November every year. We came second in the under elevens age group. Yay!

Me and my friends at pony club

Ashleigh

Emma

Me

Isabelle

We have a canteen at pony club. The mums, dads and grandparents help out and serve the food. I always get a hot dog and a soft drink.

For her lunch, Chance always gets hay and a bucket of water.

Chance and her friend, Pumpkin, eating their lunch.

Lunch time! Yay!

1.00pm to 2.00pm
Games

Games are heaps of fun! Our instructor always puts us into teams and we race against each other.

First we do the BENDING RACE. That's where we bend our horses in and out of poles and try to beat the other riders.

Next is the FLAG RACE, where we have to put a flag into a barrel, take another one out and give it to the next rider.

The last game is the STEPPING STONES race, where we get off our ponies and step over stepping stones as fast as we can. Then we have to get on really quickly and race to the finish line. Sometimes people get on too quickly and end up sitting on their pony's rump instead of the saddle!!

ME DOING THE STEPPING STONES RACE

REMEMBER!!

Ponies love a pat and a cuddle, especially after they have worked hard.

Chance and me jumping a jump called 'double trouble'!

JUMPING ON THE CROSS COUNTRY COURSE IS ALWAYS EXCITING!

The jumps have been built in a big paddock and are about 100 metres apart. Our instructor usually spends some time taking us over a few jumps before she lets us jump on our own.

A map of the cross country course at my pony club.

7. ramp

sharp turn

creek crossing

steep bank up

6. tyres

8. water jump

5. ditch

9. gate

4b. double trouble 4a.

3. steep bank down

10. brush

11. frame

2. picket fence

1. log

finish

start

Riders go over the course one at a time. We are allowed to canter pretty fast between each jump.

The jumps are all really different. They can be logs, or ditches or picket fences.

Sometimes they aren't really jumps at all but a steep hill to go up or down, or a creek to go through.

Isabelle, jumping the picket fence on the cross country course.

3.00pm Go Home

At 3.00 pm Chance and I ride home. We are both really tired. I always give Chance a special treat: pony mix (her favourite)! Then I go inside and have a nice hot bath!

Different Kinds of Horses

There are heaps and heaps of different kinds of horses but I am only going to tell you about five. They are Arabs, Quarter horses, Welsh Mountain ponies, thoroughbreds and Andalusians. Chance is part Arab and part Welsh Mountain pony.

Arabs

Arabs were first bred in Arabia and were ridden across the deserts. They have great stamina (that means they can keep on going and going and don't get tired) and courage. They are very beautiful to look at and are also known for their loving natures. They are usually between 14.2 and 15.2 hands high.

Andalusians

Andalusians are very beautiful riding horses. They were first bred in Spain and are usually grey or white. They stand about 15.2 hands high and have very thick manes and tails. They are known for their kind natures and their willingness to learn.

Quarter Horses

Quarter horses were first bred in America. They were called Quarter horses because they were very fast over a quarter of a mile. They are usually between 14 and 15.2 hands high. Quarter horses are known for their strong chest and shoulders. They are used for 'working' and roping cattle because they are quick and have calm natures.

Thoroughbreds

Thoroughbreds were bred to go very fast over long distances. They are usually fine-boned horses and most of them are over 16 hands. Today's race horses are thoroughbreds. If a thoroughbred horse is not fast enough for racing, they are often used as a jumping or dressage horse.

Welsh Mountain Ponies

Welsh Mountain ponies were first bred in Wales where it is very cold in winter so they had to be hardy. They are known for their strength and intelligence. They are great ponies for kids and are very loving. They do not grow any taller than 14 hands.

Why don't you make your
own scrapbook about horses?
It's heaps of fun!
Luv Becky x